D1531287

By the same author

Poetry
Devastating Beauty
Rumours of Light

Devotionals
Darkling: An Advent Journey

NAMING GOD

Poems

by
Gideon Heugh

For the aching

CONTENTS

Part II: Entanglement

Part III: Doing God's work

Part IV: Harmony

Part V: Epiphany

Coda: Return

NAMING GOD

Prelude

IF YOU ARE GOING
TO BELIEVE

If you are going to believe

Look to the here-life;
see that living is now;
know that you, that we, belong here.

If you are going to believe,
believe in this world;
believe in goodness, regardless.

If you are looking for facts,
wrap your heart around these:
life is painful precious, it is gorgeous, it is a gift.

Ecology

It is becoming clear to me
that the health of my bone marrow
has something to do with cornflowers,
and constellations, and the way
that a dragonfly moves.
I cannot now help but believe
(and I have explored the options)
that the motions of my soul
depend in some way upon the moon,
and the weight of clouds,
and the migratory pattern of swifts.
The flow of my consciousness is reliant
(I am increasingly certain)
upon the cleanliness of chalk streams,
the societies of protozoa in the soil,
and of course the wellbeing
of my neighbour.

Part I

REVERIE

The wheel of the year

Leaves of heart, notions of budding
against the night. Grief arrives
on the turn, and back.
All of the promises of blossom in the world
won't stop the hurt. So we wait,
and we see. Chiff chaff, blackbird,
snowdrop symbols of so much life
here and gone and then
a memory, a hope. Skies that lighten
will darken, will lighten, again.

Spring is becoming

Spring is becoming,
and the sap is on the move.
Thoughts acquire new muscle of green;
forget-me-nots are blooming—
the infinite made urgent.

Let us give thanks to the winter as it passes;
let us kneel before the primroses
and think of death. Without it,
where all this life?

Adoration for Imbolc

Hail the quickening of the year;
hail the growing curve showing
on the belly of the earth;
hail the beginning, the dawn-heart singing,
the gorgeous expectancy that the earth
will say amen to the new.

Early morning, March

You wake up anxious. Sleep was a respite,
but now your worries are pouring down your throat.
Somehow you breathe.
Somehow you get out of bed and make coffee.
You try not to face the day,
but instead go to your room and close the door.

The year is insistent in its turning;
already the world can feel the nudge of spring.
Six a.m. and you dare to pull back the curtain.
There is a glow on the horizon.
You switch off your light, clutch your warm cup,
stare into the repenting dark.

The dawn never hurries; it is too sure of itself.
You open the window, despite the cold,
and lyric of blackbird and robin pours in. The sky
slowly weaves a story. You may struggle
to agree with it, but you cannot prevent a word
like beautiful
from seeping into your blood.

The tears are from pain, yes,
but something else besides.
You woke up anxious. You are facing the day.

Afraid for the world on a
spring morning

There is pink in the sky, the blackbirds
are singing; and the plants are throwing forth
new green. Understand this: the ripening buds
on the camellia are not mere hints.
Yes the planes are bellowing overhead;
yes the boney rope of terror is tightening
around the world; yes my soul is battered and weary
and I am hardly without blame.

But see: the trees are silhouetted
against quite the shade of blue;
the wrens and the robins are presenting the case
for life; and fear is not alone in my blood
(coffee and the word are waking me up)—
under the pink bloom of the sky
I am deciding to go on.

April

April, and the weary eyes are being eased
by blossom-light. In the woods,
the ground is prepared for enchantments
of cowslip and bluebell. Christ here
is a dandelion clock, the vixen licking
the blood from her cub, the high wind
bringing the long-wintered home.

Spring does not ask for your faith,
only your presence.
Here is the month of the green tide turning,
the stem and bud's urgent sky-yearning,
the awakening earth proving
that resurrection is no fluke.

Magnolia

The air today is spring,
and sunlight is nudging
the long asleep.

After grey months
of breathing in
only cold, now the wary souls
are filled bright
with magnolia.

It is easy

It is easy
in the spring
for God
to be heard

from the hedges
come the voices
of the wren
and the blackbird.

Beltane

The bluebells are kindling dream-talk
in the shade of the deepwood.
In at least one garden (we pray)
a child is putting their hands
in the earth; is discovering root
and worm and beetle.

Not all the fires of beginning
flare bright. Before sunrise
(it has to be before sunrise)
we go to the grass and wash our faces
in May's first fall of dew; we praise
the darkful sky who brought it.

Spring blessing

Trip your sagging heart
into the vernal gleam;
foot-light that weary body
through the wood-flowers' desiring breath.
Life is becoming (it will
become you).

Heaven is in a mood
and the blackthorn is showing it;
sap-shifts and chaffinches
and good God
have you seen the primroses?

In this light

Look here. In this light there may be
(I saw today the cloud-clearing blossom,
the rinse of flowers upon my eyes)—
it could all be new.

It is easy yesterday to be filled with wonder,
and now of course we are all so tired.
But in this light the longing will get to you.
It simply has to.

Do not let your pain become a smear.
Breathe in the sky—drink the pink petal
and the leaf. In this greening of the air
the questions (God how I wish there were answers)
could be leading you somewhere.

You could say that heaven is lustful
of flowers

It is flesh that we want.
God has no interest in being only a mind.
Resting in the shade of a mulberry tree,
Christ would listen to the sea
as it breathed upon the shore.
Often he would go alone into the hills
and watch the bees dipping themselves
into the lips of the wildflowers.
As the sparrows and warblers sang the dawn,
he would cook breakfast for his friends—
body bright with the smell of smoke and bread
and the sound of idle, happy talk.

Our great thirst is incarnation.
Repentance is an embodiment, a return
to interconnection at the level of our heartbeats.
All around us life and all its fullness
is beckoning—the flowers are opening themselves
saying come to me, and drink.

Lines for a morning in May

Every morning is a veil
torn in two. Hear its chorus
swell, elevate—its lyrics all proof
and elixir; sooth of song and light.
Here we dip into gentler time,
life itself as balm, nature bringing you home,
a reminder that it includes you.

We make ourselves springful of God
by remembering the fleshness of things.
We notice our incarnation, embodied
in this larger body.
Here we unlearn our heresy
by losing ourselves in the flowers,
in the movement of butterflies,
in the scent of spring rain.

Here we are hopeful,
not through some promise
that it will all get better
(though you never know),

but through the simple truth
of beauty's unfolding.

You don't have to chase after meaning—
you just have to sit still long enough
to notice it.

Even May, in all its urgency, is more lovely
by repose.
So gorgeous, this life, this world,
that despite our most anxious fractures
it speaks unquestionably of love.

The cold dew

There are some things that clearly
you are not meant to know:
why the blackcap waits so long
to join the dawn chorus, holding his moment
until the day is more obvious;
why the tears do not always arrive
when you think they should,
but linger inside you until a small tenderness
loosens their will; why God, shrouded
in our assumptions, ignores your call,
deciding instead to walk through the morning,
to feel the cold dew on his toes.

August poem

The breath of August is a gentle astonishment:
the plumpness of blackberries,
the lush purpose of the fields,
the swell of butterflies
as they make music of the wildflowers.
In late summer, you wouldn't be surprised
to find the fullness of Christ
in a blackthorn, or a damselfly,
or the noise of lifefulness
in the long grass.

Reverie

We are redeemed by reverie.
There are no paths
through the strange woods
of our thoughts. It is only by wandering
that we find what we need—
steps slurred by daydream
until our hearts are transformed
by an idea about trees.

Come with me

Come with me, for the night is quick with wonder;
come with me, and together let's break our hesitancy
upon the stars.

So what if our sighs are deeper
than they used to be?
So what if the lines on our faces
tell stories we would rather forget?
Let's grab our coats
and hang them on the crescent moon;
let's swim through the songful rivers of the dark
until our flesh is silvered with belonging;
let's surrender to the pull of wild calling to wild,
hearts urging themselves on
while the heavens dote upon our dreams.

Come with me, and be more midnight
with your yearning;
life is all manner of enchantment—
here we can let go of any thought
of breaking the spell.

Walking

When I walk, I think.
Well, our minds are always busy
with something; but when I walk, I think.

It's like this: at the beginning of the pandemic,
when we all stayed at home,
the word came out of Venice
that the waters had become clear.
You could see all the way through.
In the absence of so much noise,
even the dolphins had returned.

When I walk, I think.
My soul becomes clear.
I can see all the way through.
In the absence of so much noise,
even hope returns.

Dawn poem

Coffee keeps me close to God
as I stand and listen
to the dawn.
How so?
Coffee keeps me awake enough
to stand and listen
to the dawn.

That twinkle in your eye (a meditation on Midsummer)

Midsummer's eve. A time when magic gathers thickly,
when light is honeyed and warm
and the dark has an aura of what-if.
The year's waning begins,
but not before the waxing's final flourish.

There is rumour of God leaping from branch to branch
in the greenwood, fey and unpredictable—
Christ-as-puck, weaving spells upon the twilighted.
You will be told unconvincingly
that it was just a dream.

Who knows what you could become when Spirit
is in this mood? Who knows what could burn away
on Midsummer's bonfire if you let it?
Cast off; leap over;
take that twinkle in your eye and run with it.

Grace is the Faerie Queen, sultry, seeking,
tasting the air to catch the scent of your yearning

so she can roll in the grass with it.
Go now with hot daring.
Go and be transformed.

Rainstorm

This rain is a mood—thunderous
and absolving, its fingers making deep music
as they reach through the leaves.

I pray for a rainstorm within me,
its refrain clean and heavy and vibrant;
a new air; life returning to life.

Part II

ENTANGLEMENT

Love is like

The universe, expanding faster than the speed of light,
making more of everything.
The deciduous souls, who know when green is good
and when it isn't.

After my heart first broke, I begged
for the anguish to stop; is it strange
that now I would not change it?
We are fortunate the tulips will not last long;
they will be back next year, and well after we are gone.

Flowers are colourful because they want more life.
Love is old fashioned; it is just a load of chemicals;
it is the marrow of Christ.
What are you believing today?

Weep and dance and laugh all you can.
The universe is expanding faster
than the speed of light—
if you keep clinging to yourself,
you won't be able to hold on.

Waking early, Teshuvah

I know that I need more sleep, far more sleep than this,
but I also know that I need to change my life.

Perhaps at this thin hour, passing ships
with our dreams,
it is quiet enough to hear our souls—
so often drowned out by the strange need to be useful.

Perhaps the smell of dew
will bring God down from the clouds
where we so zealously put him to work.

I know that I need more sleep,
but the songs that greet the first breath of day
sound like repentance.
So what of bleary eyes if waking early
lets me remember something about grace?

Angels are more interested in our yearnings
than our ambitions.
Take those deeper sighs

and cast them upon morning's altar—
you might find that you are not alone.

Do not be troubled by this stirring,
these aches of divinity
returning your blood to meaning.

I know that I need more sleep,
but during the day
I am too busy asking
to receive,
too busy thinking
to be thoughtful,
too busy trying to make a living
to remember to be alive.

I am here now, awash with dawn's soft clarity.

The mercy of this world's abundance.
I will go and change my life.

No one should pretend

I don't want to give you the wrong impression.
No one should pretend
that it's all miracles and hydrangeas
and blackbird song in the deep leaves.
Life, for many (all too many) days
is a terror, or a sorrow.

Azure dragonflies, a message from a friend,
a wave of sunlight crashing into your heartbreak
can change the course of your soul,
but not always.

Not every sunrise brings epiphany.
Today was little more than doomscrolling
and sobbing into a cup of tea.
But it will be okay in the end. Maybe.

Atonement

You wonder if the ground will forgive us.
When the High Priest trembled
inside the Holy of Holies, forever was not a chemical
being sprayed onto the grass,
there were no microplastics in the soil
or in a newborn's heart;
there were countless trees, clean air to breathe;
he could not have imagined the firmament
being choked by our greed.

We can do the work of atonement.
We can, perhaps, heal
and return to our souls.
But what if it is too late
to repair the world?
You wonder if the ground will forgive us.

Lament for the trees

Where now the easeful whisper of the leaves?
Where now the birds nesting hope
in the high canopy?
Where now the bough dripping careful light
onto the ground?

Where now the bend
that breaks through the storm?
Where now the web of roots
making sense of being?
Where now the gentle-strong stretch
towards becoming?

I hear the scream of our self-imposed isolation.
I feel the splits in the flesh of God.
I see the fall, the body of our home
unable to rise.

Android

How often have my daughter's eyes
gone searching for my own—
her gentle heart reaching out to mine
to be met only by my phone?

I sincerely hope

I sincerely hope that something within you
snaps—that the final straw
lands upon your soul
and you fly into a rage
about how much they have stolen your attention;
how they have made you believe
in acclaim, in busyness, in accumulation.
I hope that you completely lose your cool—
that the weight of individualism
and materialism
and endless comparison
breaks your patience, and that in a sudden rush
of aliveness you decide
to burn the whole thing down.

After therapy

I am told to go easy. To take my time.
Let all those losses settle back
into the under-you.
Let all that pain run out of breath,
return to the comfortable nooks
in which it normally dwells.
And those sharp secrets you revealed—
the ones that keep you huddled
in glooms of shame—
put them back, carefully.
Then you can carry on with who you were
before: one who is held in,
quaking in some depth but at least presentable,
at least able to get through
what might be called a day.

When I am dying

When I am dying, I read a poem.
I walk to the deli and buy a sandwich—
roast pork, stuffing, plenty of butter and apple sauce.
When I am dying, I turn off the TV;
I think of throwing it away.
I go to the woods with my daughter;
we make up silly games.
When I am dying, I tell the truth,
no matter how much it costs.
I spend time with people who make me laugh—
people who aren't afraid to hug, to kiss,
to shed tears over broken dreams.
When I am dying, I stop scrolling;
I drop the busyness; I shake my head
at the idea of success.
I might listen to the rain; luxuriate in a bookshop;
slowly prepare a table for lunch.
When I am dying, I write a poem;
I try to remember what it means to be alive.

The thermodynamics of grief

You are gone. Thirteen billion years
and now this. Energy cannot be created
or destroyed, only changed, so I cannot understand
how, when you left,
all the light left with you.

We are the centre of nothing.
If we were never here, the universe would have
expanded
regardless. Why then, in your sudden absence,
does the whole thing now seem
so small?

Cutting roses as my daughter sings to
the thunder

Late summer, and we are dream-hazing
through the day: honey drizzled over slices
of crisp apple; idle conversation
about the graces of moss; flour and giggles everywhere
as we roll out dough for pizza.
We watch Bambi, and talk to each other about fear.

In the evening you ride your scooter
and we hear a few dark notes of thunder.
You fall, and I hold you until you can get up again.
We see faint drops of distant lightning,
counting the seconds until its voice cannons over us.
I tell you that the storm is far away,
but that it's still okay to be scared.

I cut the roses, glancing over my shoulder
as you ride beneath the gathering clouds.
You are singing to them, asking them to go
somewhere else. We ask ourselves if the thunder
is their own song. It begins to rain.

. . .

Before we go inside, you tell me that you speak
to the bees. 'What do they say?'
'That they love the flowers. That sometimes
they are afraid.'

The sunflowers (for Ukraine)

In the shattered fields;
in the cities where the lovers
and the widows lay down;
in the old stories and the new blood
dripping onto soil and street—
there the seeds are waiting.

Do not doubt the flowers
will reach again
towards the sun;
do not doubt
they will outlast the hatred.

There will be peace when
(after Etty Hillesum)

There will be peace when
every human being
(yes you, yes me)
reaches into their heart
finds the prejudice
the hatred
the unyieldingness
that is there
(believe me, it is there)
and does everything they can
to remove it.

Firmament

Slumped in the bathroom, two a.m.,
heart crumpling beneath the weight
of its own failures.
I know there is a mirror.
I do not want to know
what it has to say.

Walk back into the bedroom
where my daughter is sleeping.
I am a hero to her.
Through the wall I can feel the mirror sneering.
I try not to sob—it would wake her up.

I peer through the curtain,
and suddenly it feels
as though I have walked over a grave.
Orion looms vast in the sky,
unfathomable in its beyonding,
and for an eternal moment
I am inhaled by the cosmos,
falling into the terror of distance.

. . .

In the firmament I am nothing.
My failures, my successes
become absurd.

My daughter stirs and I am regrounded.

Then I try something.
Turning back to the stars
I hold up the love that I have for her.
There is a change.
Now I am the colossus,
and Orion is no giant,
and all the sky seems small,
and all the mirrors are breaking.
I try not to sob.

Where it all leads

The news chokes my heart. The grief
makes me sick.

> *The sun rises, I discover*
> *a brand new shade of light.*

Pain. Why always
so much pain? I am afraid.

> *A piano. Debussy. No one can say*
> *why there should be anything gorgeous*
> *at all.*

The planet is dying.
Our descendants will hate us.

> *Two people meet for the first time.*
> *They will become lovers.*

The sadness is a whole universe
being born in my chest.

. . .

An acorn falls to the ground. Oak whispers
a hundred years from now.

Heartbreak. Anxiety.
Christ knows it will ever stop.

The children are at play. Laughing.
I cannot help but smile.

The wise do not try to explain suffering.
Just let us hurt, they say.

It leaves me breathless to think
that spring will come regardless.

All that loss. Hopes crushed.
Where does love leave us?

The sun rises. Shout at the Earth
but you won't stop it from turning.

Rain

Aware of the weariness,
aware of the pain,
aware of the heart hung low
I step out into the rain.

See what happens when a body finds itself in step
with the intent of the earth;
see what happens when the sky
is no longer a concept
but is brushing against your skin.

Now all that has been held
is washing into the drains,
is making its way to the sea,
is being broken up
by the waves.

And now the chaffinch is singing,
and now I am able to lift my heart,
and I am aware that if I desired
I could be broken up too.

The light of the world

The light of the world
is the smile against all odds;
it is the tears that bring relief;
it is the decision to go on,
the painful right above the easy wrong,
the wide-eyed love
instead of blind belief.

Hope

Despair feels comfortable.
Giving up is all too easy.
There is little required of you
when you believe that everything is lost.

Hope, on the other hand, is fearsome
in its demands. It insists upon you,
lifting you from the soft bed of inaction,
burning the command into your bones
that there is work to be done.

The facts

Perhaps today we will lift our hearts from the fog
and begin to think of life. Perhaps today
we will stop scrolling past it,
distracting ourselves from it,
shuffling our soul away from its aches
in favour of light entertainment.

There is a weight here.
You cannot know if it is one worth bearing
unless you stop to pick it up.
Come down with me now
to life. Come with me
and face the facts.

My grandmother spent her last decade
in a care home. Lonely, hardly able
to walk, or talk. I was too lazy, too distracted
to visit her as often as I should. I would never know
what to say, and would never stay very long.

. . .

The things we would do differently.
The chances we will never get.

Feed your soul on the ache.
Stop scrolling past it.

My daughter's laughter heals me of myself.
I won't always be able to keep her safe;
she won't always need me this much.
When I dreamt so long of fatherhood,
I wasn't thinking of grief.

Come with me
and face the facts.

Your experiences are not unusual. We love people
who feel nothing for us at all. The sun sets
and there only terror.

Yet perhaps you have seen sunrises
that have mended the world.
Perhaps you have held a hand
and felt the pulse of God.

. . .

There have been moments when I have done little
but dance, or play silly games, or sit quietly on a chair
gazing dozily at the roses
thinking how blessed, how very blessed we are.

Lines in defence of an
un-augmented reality

1

Let's start with the basics, like the fact
that we have been given lips to kiss with

(a pause here to dwell on this, and smile
that smile—you know the one I mean).

There isn't much that a machine could tell you
about the taste of your lover's skin,
or the way the night sky feels
as it sings into your eyes,
or how love is all ache and miracle
and softness and anguish.

Could anything other than a soul
tell you why grief is worth it?

2

A screen can do a lot of things,
but this morning, as my daughter and I

counted the different types of bee
visiting the lavender, I swear
that out of the corner of my eye
I could see Christ stretching out upon the grass.

An app can improve your productivity,
but do not mistake that for improving your life.

Remember how much you laughed that night?
Remember how that sunrise
made you want to change your mind?
Remember how good that homemade cheesecake was?

There is no substitute for looking into their eyes.
You can neither replace nor imitate the thumb
that brushes the tear away from your cheek,
or the healing that slowly comes
when you take yourself into the more green
and brightening airs
(and that beautiful discovery—
that you too are part of this luminosity).

3
You look to the dawn, and music is drifting

from the trees, and the horizon is a sigh of hope,
and any time that you like
you could tell someone that you love them.
Do not let anything convince you
that this gift we have is not enough.

I know you will have shared a meal with friends
and thought, 'This is what life is about.'
Friend, this is what life is about.

The sages tell us that the spiritual journey
is one of subtraction.
If only we would stop burying the immensities
beneath layers of augmentation.

When hate seems to be winning

Take the stones out of your breath.
Reach for the hands of your sorrow—
we need all the soul we can get. Turn away
from the parts of you that are certain of anything
but the need for grief, and kindness, and the belief
that change, even amid the cruelty and the horror
and the anguish, is possible.
When other hearts are shrinking, make yours larger.
Take the side of humanity—
bless as much of it as you can.
See if your compassion can go further
than your pain wants to let you;
there are always ways to help, however small.
If you are going to withdraw
(and no one could blame you)
withdraw into softness, into the arms of goodness,
which though they do not seem it, are now;
are endless.

Part III

DOING GOD'S WORK

And what is it that I want to achieve?

To write, with pencil or pen, each moment
so slowly—each letter, each word so lucid
with feeling—that life cannot help
but be a poem.

To know, simply in my nature,
where I might find a particular star
on a particular night; the phase of the moon;
what the roots make of it.

To make learnings of stillness, quiet;
to take their lessons to heart and to pray
so unobtrusively, so entirely present,
that the dawnbirds come to feed out of my hand.

The ecstasy of no

I rejected
the offer
with pleasure.

Praise the ecstasy
of no—
it is syrup
in the mouth

it allows me
to lie down
with a book.

Boxes

Proudly, I brought before God
a box of accomplishment—years in the making.
But on the divine countenance I saw
only a look of pity, and exasperation
(not, however, without love).
I was told to put my effort aside,
then was given another box.
'How many times do I need to tell you?
You are meant to fill it with life!'

Dancing

If I find that I have too many ideas
about the soul
I pour myself a drink, I make sure
that I am barefoot, I put on some music
and begin to move—

—I get out of my head
and into my limbs, all the unnecessary forgotten
as feet and heartbeat
remember the truth.

Here

It is here that we find our forever. Here,
in our saying yes to this world, to now,
to the realm of each other. It is here, untethered
from the future and so many ideas
of ourselves, that we find our forever.

Today, I walked through the halls of trees
where we came in the early days of the pandemic.
It is here that I taught you to embrace the pines,
and I marvelled at you, finding your feet
in the dappled light. I remember your laughter
as I skipped beside you—you
all wonder and joy as you toddled along—
the breath of the woods and your smile
dissolving me into the heart
of what this might all be about:

Life cannot merely make sense after the fact.
It is here that we find our forever;
here, in this world, in the realm of each other.

To do less

There will always be too much
to do, so your greatest hope
is to do less—reject the hustle, the grind,
the furious race to achieve and acquire things
that death will reveal to be useless.

Come to your senses
and be deliciously un-busy.
You can make the most of time
not by squeezing it, but by letting it go.
Give yourself to the little things.
No success ever held as much joy
as the first bluebell in spring,
the sweet sorrows of autumn,
or the warmth of a hand on your shoulder.

This

Sugared scent of buddleia;
hum of bumbles among the marigold
and the cornflower;

falling light; settling quiet;
a question
drifting
through the warmly air.

'This,'
replies my soul.

Blessed

Blessed are the ones who say no.
Blessed are the ones who think that living
is ambition enough.
Blessed are the simple, the gentle, the unsung.

Heaven tastes bitter to the overachiever.
It belongs to the children, and to the ones
who despite the gnawing aspiration of years
have not forgotten what it means be to delighted.

Blessed are the ones who walk slowly,
who would get distracted by a daisy,
who would rather climb a tree than a ladder.

Doing God's work

It was an idle kind of day.
I sat in the garden for unmarked time,
watching the trees; watching the light
hovering among the leaves.
Later, I ate honey
spread thickly on bread.
I drank, slowly, a cold glass
of wine. I lay down
knowing that I had done God's work,
knowing that all was sanctified.

A guide to the Sabbath

It is not doing nothing, although it could be.
It is not mere happiness, although who can say
for sure? Certainly you shouldn't think anything
of piety.

How are you feeling? The answer is less important
than the fact you are asking yourself the question.

It's not about rules, but here's an idea:
no one ever rested with their eyes on a phone.
This is a day to ruin your busyness—
to expose it as a scam.

What will it take to make you sink into your depths?
How can you remind yourself that you have them?

Think of what your hands could be doing.
The more body the better.
Think of food prepared with love, and shared.
Think of what brings your truest smile,
or your most contended sigh.

. . .

You don't have to feel guilty at all.

Don't look up what the weather is doing. Go into it.
Don't neglect your ache, use it
to break your way into aliveness.
Yearn yourself into the heart of what truly matters.

Throw off thoughts of when and then.
This, maybe, is what it's all for:
if you're not here, you're not anywhere.

Heaven is not the sum of anything

Heaven is not the sum of anything.
All that striving, all that accumulation
answers in zero.
No amount of belief adds up to abundance.

Love and wonder cannot be grasped—
they are fallen into.
Spirit turns away
from the white knuckle.

The summer garden

A book in my lap, the morning sun
pooling upon the ink, spilling
onto the ground as I lift the pages, occasionally,
to read. There is just enough of a breeze
to make the birches and the pines
speak to the wren; just enough
to carry the scent of the roses
to my shoulders, so that if I tilt my head
just a little, I can brush it with my cheek.

The day leans back, stretches out its legs.
There is much that could be said
about buttercups, and lavender,
and the colour of the sky. But in my ease,
it all falls into one. Thinking back,
I do not know if it was the wren singing,
or if it was the roses.

Continuums of soulfulness

All that noise pervading you—
all the scrolling, the browsing, the endless
rushing around—no wonder your soul
has crawled beneath your bones;
no wonder it doesn't want to come out.

Distraction pushes the whispers of your heart
outside of your awareness;
busyness crowds the space within you
until your spirit curls up into a ball.

Yet in stillness you can arrive, slowly,
at the truths of yourself.
In returning to quietude time after time
you can begin to gain the trust of your shy depths.

Let your being breathe.
Make space for time; make time for space;
create continuums of soulfulness.
Put Sabbath at the centre of your life
and you will find that your life becomes centred.

. . .

For how can you learn
The gorgeous secrets of your soul
If you never stop to listen?

Well-rested

There are creams you can buy
which when put around your eyes
give you the appearance of being
well-rested.
But here is some advice
(and it might save your life)
you could just try being
well-rested.

Slow

Rushed has no power
in the garden,
in the hushening meadow,
in the breathful wood.

Slow heals,
gentle restores,
idle is good.

Rushed has no power
in the soul,
in the aching heart,
in the mind tormented by could and should.

Slow heals,
gentle restores,
idle is good.

Part IV

HARMONY

In the mud

When the sky god failed me,
I buried myself gut first
in the mud. That is where I felt the roots
and the worms
like fingers
reaching for me.

All that time wanting to soar
like an eagle, not realising
that in the clouds
nothing grows.

The dark of my heart

Here are the unheard exhalations of my soul.
Here is the breath of God (the audacity of life, dreams
of a love that is greater than forever)
forever inside of my trembling.

Here is the dark of my heart,
now somehow shining.

Here is the unconceivable belief
that I am not the encompass of my disaster,
that there is (no, I am not ready to name it)
that I am here
with You
alive in all my weakness.

Notes from the Holy Land

A rabbi says: joy should not dance alone;
neither, indeed, should sadness.
You must invite them both into the circle.

At the Western Wall, a man tells me
the way I ought to be praying
and then asks me for some money.
Barukh atah Adonai Eloheinu,
Melekh ha`olam.

On the beaches of Tel Aviv,
young people watch the sun
bleed into the sea
as it lowers itself from heaven.
On the 3 a.m. streets, a woman screams
to her boyfriend that she's tired of the lies.
All he can do is cry out her name.
Barukh atah Adonai Eloheinu,
Melekh ha`olam.

A girl called Grace tells me

that she hates religion,
but that she can't ignore
the transcendence she felt
after eating some magic mushrooms.
Barukh atah Adonai Eloheinu,
Melekh ha`olam.

In Nazareth, I weep
over an icon of Mary from Ukraine.
A little later, I haggle with a vendor
over the price of a Tree of Life necklace.
Around the corner, the words 'Fuck Israel'
have been sprayed onto a wall.
Barukh atah Adonai Eloheinu,
Melekh ha`olam.

It is three days since 13 children
were blown up in Gaza.
On Haram al-Sharif, a crowd
hoist a cloth-wrapped body into the air
shouting again and again
that God is great.
Barukh atah Adonai Eloheinu,
Melekh ha`olam.

. . .

Waist deep in the Jordan river,
a man named Samuel
is quivering with pain as he tells me
how he hasn't seen his daughter
in months; about how his ex-wife
had just gotten remarried.
We plunge each other seven times
into the water
as the fish nibble on our dead skin.
Barukh atah Adonai Eloheinu,
Melekh ha`olam.

In a Jerusalem youth hostel, I am watching
a group of Arab and Jewish strangers
learning to dance the blues.
Barukh atah Adonai Eloheinu,
Melekh ha`olam.

A tour guide asks me
why I have the word Holy
tattooed on my wrist.

Five meditations: a year when Passover
and Good Friday fall on the same day

1

Blake wondered if the lamb knew anything of God.
Who can say? But it knows the fragrance
of the bright April grass; it knows the sweet warmth
of its mother's milk; and it knows the dark fear
of the snarling dogs.

2

I have killed no lamb today, but I get the idea.
In the garden, heavy rain has spoiled most
of the magnolia's white flowers. But there is one left
that is quite perfect. I slice through its green neck
and place it upon the table inside.

3

All that blood on the doorposts.
I wonder if they heard the angel of death
as it crawled through the streets beyond their doors.
I wonder how much guilt they felt
amid the screams of that long dawn.

. . .

On the news today, more children blown to pieces
by bombs. Little flower, fragile scent;
I look at the sky above me.

Tavener knew what he was doing—
religious music should be haunted by minors.
Christ said that the heavenly realm
belongs to such as these.

4

At the Seder, the young ones chant
*Why is this night different? Why do we eat
the bitter herbs? Why do the grown ones
swallow God's words with glass after glass of wine?*

I do not want to waste my life, and such reminders
are useful. We should know where death is;
we should know that from time to time
the skies grow dark.

5

Who can say if Jesus truly thought he was forsaken?

As each spring fades, God presses her face
into to the flowers and breathes deeply.

They will bloom again next year;
it does not stop her from weeping.

Pirkei Avot 2:15-16

It is true, the odds are stacked against us.
It is true, the weight of the world feels
as though it may break us.

Our days are numbered;
the clock is ticking;
and the goodness on which we wanted to depend
too often seems to go missing.

Do not be afraid—
to complete the repair of the world
is not why you were made.
You were created to play
only your part; whatever is within your hands;
whatever is the now of your heart.

One of the problems we have is

We keep expecting God
to be lording on the clouds
when she's treely in the greenwood
dreaming roots into the ground.

If you weren't so obliged

'I just can't feel God's presence!'

Have you felt the morning sun
on your face?

'I just can't hear God's voice!'

Have you heard the music of the skylark
in spring?

'I just don't know what God wants with me!'

And what would you do
if you weren't so obliged?

The longings of heaven

God is not that interested
in how often you read the Bible—
how often you say the Lord's prayer.
Closer to the top of the longings of heaven
is whether or not you know the fragrance
of healthy soil, and why it matters.
Learning scripture is one thing,
but would you know a yellowhammer's song
if you heard it? Do you know that their numbers
are declining, and why it matters?

You can go to church, you can perform
the rites, but these are only a small part
of the body of Christ.
In the oceans, the corals have been bleached;
in the woods, there are far fewer moths
than there ought to be;
and in your soul, there is a space
that will only expand
if you listen to the rumours of the trees—
if you know why they matter.

Matthew 10:7

And this is what the rabbi said:
'As you live, proclaim with your life
that heaven is shockingly intimate.
Its arms are wrapped around you—
not a distant promise, not mere imminence,
but the audaciously ordinary.
It is breathing now upon you;
it is urging you to join in.'

Easter Sunday

Easter Sunday, and spring warmth
is easing itself upon the lavender,
delighting the always-Christ in me.
Far away indoors, the priests (anxious
for souls) proclaim news of bloody atonement.
Choose the right god (our god), they say,
and thanks to unconditional grace
—wait—you too can escape from hellfire.

Unconcerned, we attend to the garden.
In the green hearts, punishment is beyond imagining;
we are all just unfurling our longing to be.
No one is alive, or dead, exclusively.
The insects, the stars, the trees made and make you.
We eat from the community of decay
that is the soil. Life happens,
beautifully, sometimes dreadfully,
and it comes to an end. And then
—wait—it begins again.

But God is a weed

In churches they give praise
to the flowers they have planted.
But God is a weed—
found most often among the neglected,
rising coarse and unlooked for
through the broken slabs, playing havoc
with our pretty borders.

What if

What the earth knew something we didn't;
what if the air was wise;
what if God was staring out
from within a child's eyes?

What if being here was the miracle;
what if you didn't need to shine;
what if the mundane was holy
and your flesh was flecked with the divine?

Harmony

The psalmist declared
that if we were silent
the rocks themselves would cry out.
They're not waiting for us.
He just wasn't listening.

Listen.
Clearly I am not the sum of my prayers,
that is unless Christ looks nothing like
what we have been taught.

Believe me. Christ
looks nothing like
what we have been taught.

Earlier in life
I had the habit of going out each night
to look at the stars. You cannot stand
beneath the chasm of the sky
and not fall out of yourself.

. . .

Are we not listening?
The original sin was believing
we could be separate from everything else.

> Many people, after being hurt,
> close themselves off.
> Why risk another loss?
> I attempt to fill my brokenness
> by dragging love into me.
> None of this works.

The word diabolical
means to throw apart.
The word disaster
means to become disconnected
from the stars.
Listen.

> Awe is a kind of salvation.

I really don't deserve all this—
to be able to show my daughter Jupiter's moons

through the same lens I first saw them.

We don't deserve it—this; all of this.
But here it is.
Doesn't that say something?
What are the stones trying to tell us?

Alone, we are godless.
Of course we're all miserable,
told over and over
that the individual is absolute.

The devil bathes in the first person.

We spend more time looking into screens
than eyes.
Slowly we are reversing
the incarnation.
Slowly we are loosening
the thread of love.

Listen. You belong here—
under the moon-song,
the tree-song,

                    the rising-sun song.
                              Listen—
                    it's all the same-song.

And if we pay attention,
we might find the harmony.

Grace

However many times I sigh with sadness;
however many years I feel crawling
beneath my skin;
however much I'm told that hope is a madness;
however much the cynic's voice takes hold within;

however many days it seems as though I waste;
however much I'm sick
of repeating the same mistakes;
even though my heart splits
and life spits
and then hits me in the face—

I can't get away from grace.
I can't get away from grace.

Kol Nidre

Let us now determine our fate.

Let us reject pious words
and instead return—
for the divine is not a rule
that can be broken;
heaven is not a law
that we can keep, or otherwise.

No, holiness is the intimacy
of this unveiled reality;
spirit is the lover, waiting patiently.

Let us now determine our fate.

Let us step back from our minds
and see what our hearts can unbreak—
casting off all that ties us
to what is strived for,
what is earned.

. . .

Let us now return—
release our intent into connection,
the oneness of a world
that demands no vows,
that is simply life
easing through its being
and the being of what love creates.

Let us return; let us determine our fate.

If

If you are grieving, or you are putting your arms around the grieving; if you are broken-hearted, or doing your best to comfort the broken-hearted; if you are oppressed, or speaking up for those who are oppressed; if you are vulnerable, or you are finding safety for the vulnerable; if you have been attacked, or you are caring for those who have been attacked; if you are suffering, or you are working to ease the hurt of the suffering; if you are terrified, or you are holding the hands of the terrified; if you are lonely, or you are reaching out to the lonely; if you are hungry, or you are feeding the hungry; if you are thirsty, or you are giving the thirsty something to drink; if you are homeless, or you are providing shelter to the homeless; if you pursue peace; if you care for this world; if you put the needs of others first; if you unclench your fist; if you love, knowing the cost—God is on your side.

Take the leap anyway

Dare to believe. And when believing lets you down,
and after you have grieved, believe in something bigger.
Keep going until all that you have faith in
is the earth, life, and everything.

Love. And when love lets you down,
and after you have grieved, take your love further.
Keep expanding the circle until all that you love
is the earth, life, and everything.

They will convince you to be cynical.
They will convince you to close up, to tighten your fist.
They will convince you that life isn't worth the risk.
Take the leap anyway.

The earth and the sky declare it

The earth and the sky declare it.
Wonder does not have to be a pursuit.
Meaning is not a treasure
to be snatched at.

The trees do not stand there for so long
for nothing. When the song thrush sings
it seems to do so with its whole body,
and more besides.

I peeked through the curtain last night
and for seemingly no reason
a thousand stars were content
to curve through my mind.

Research suggests that acts of kindness
are a better treatment for depression than therapy.
You think we would have figured it out by now.
So many centuries since Galileo,
but still we misplace the revolution.

. . .

To be awed is a choice.
Are we willing to look around?

A social media post speaks of unleashing the divine
within. Fine, but
you could be empowered like nothing else
and still be lonely as hell.

Love is a web. A thread on its own
will do nothing.

Love is the leap of faith
that shows the chasm was never there.
If only we believed in entanglement—
instead we are sold self-care.

How different are you really from the tree,
or the song thrush, or the star? Assume nothing.

Put up a wall and you are less alive.
The first shall be last
because they have left everyone else behind.

All God asks

God does not require your belief;
God does not need to be defended;
God does not profit from being championed
in the stale halls of right-ness.

All God asks
is that we uncover our hearts and eyes—
which will lead us to awareness—
which will lead us to wonder—
which will lead us to gratitude—
which will lead us to humility—
which will lead us to compassion—
which will lead us to justice—
which will lead us to the healing of the world.

Do *not be afraid*

Death is coming for you, cold
and illuminating. Its hands will one day stretch
towards the people you love.
Do not be afraid.

You will never get everything done.
You will fail, and be humiliated.
It is possible that your dreams will not come true.
Do not be afraid.

Life will never be exhausted of wonder.
It will always hold the possibility of terror.
There will be times when you cannot help
but feel joy; when you cannot help
but feel afraid.

Do not be afraid.

Naming God

God is death, and what death becomes.

God is the pale blue of morning—
light growing in response to itself.

God is the sobs of the young lover;
the dust flung off by swirling galaxies;
the twinkle in the eye of the aging dreamer.

God is the wonder that aches into you
when you lift your eyes towards the stars;
the contentment welling up inside of you
as you lower your hands into the soil.

The turn of the seasons; the ripening
and the decay; the wild laughter
and the frightening tears and the sorrow that's kissed
by a smile.

God is the hope that you set aside
nonetheless following you.

. . .

God is the dark space in the margins of cathedrals;
the breeze searching the quiet meadow;
the question that's lurking beneath an easy answer.

God is the slow motions of grief;
love—its gentle tenacities.

God is the weeping space
where the trees used to be;
the anger of the violated;
the tenacious stem of justice.

God is the long miracle.

God is the artist who almost gave up;
the secret that only disappointment can reveal.

God is the fire
painting great shadows
of our smallness.

God is whatever it is

that makes us think we should dance.

God is the purpose of the worm;
the song of the bird that eats it;
the wiry limbs of the fox that kills the bird—
the fox whose body
will be taken by the worm.

God is the refusal to be cynical;
the people who decide to help;
the long-buried seed touched
by a whisper of warmth.

God is the unfathomability of meaning;
the knowledge that it means something beautiful
anyway.

God is simplicity itself.

God is what pulls you towards other souls;
the quivering web of existence;
the first and the last gasps
of creation.

Part V

EPIPHANY

Creation

The Talmud says both
that the world was created in spring
and that it was created in autumn.

We begin in the bright dawn;
we begin in the dark gasp of nightfall.
Hope arrives like the green of a new bud;
it arrives like the withering of leaves.

To be born anew, end afresh;
to turn to a new chapter, conclude
the one you have been reading.

The world is created in spring;
the world is created in autumn.

Notes on the first days of Autumn

Bees carry the last of the honey-dust
through the paling, goldling light.
The horse-chestnuts are heavy with their fruit,
while ahead of their sleep the roses
make their final bloom,
and are no less lovely for it.
The dawn air has the beginning
of a crunch to it; mist-breath
won't be far behind.

Chord progressions of sorrow
are resolved in autumn.
Here the harmonies start to make sense.
Here you realise that sadness is not grey,
that the lossful air has a sweetness to it.
Now is the time to gather in.
Collect yourself, bring it home—
a windfallen bundle in your arms.
We can dream of kicking through the leaves.
We can plan short, circular walks.
We can make preserves.

Acorn

I thumb the acorn
into the soft ground
then cover it
with a little soil.

Dreams dote on me, and I wait there
for several months.

The green stem
breathes out of the earth—sunlight
both new and memory.
I wait again, this time for longer,
this time until well after
I am dead.

I look up at the oak tree,
smile,
and nod my head.

Autumn

And so nature, weary from holding
the summer's luscious measure,
folds into the ground,
lays her head down,
slows and deepens her breath.

Beloved, would that you learn from her
and fall into the sacredness of rest.

Life, in all its falling

The leaves are trying to tell you
that you needn't be afraid of change;
that the only true disaster
is when we refuse to put things
in the ground.

I went to listen to the trees today,
and in the midst of all the loss
I heard this sound: life, in all its falling,
promising to be born again.

Autumn soup

We walk the lanes, our breath before us,
the earth and the sun at grateful angles.
The ease of your steps, the brightness in your eyes
is a lesson. Hands held, laughter, taking time as it is—
the being here that makes life worth the trouble.

Each day is new colour in the leaves.
We point this out to each other,
cross the roads carefully.
There is little purpose to our strolling,
nor should there be. The delight of this world
is gratuitous; the design of beauty merely
to be beautiful.
I don't need to tell my daughter how glorious this is.

We stumble upon the chestnuts,
hundreds of them, a new ground,
some of them split open in invitation.
I show you how to avoid most of the spikes
(you can't get around getting hurt completely)
and we fill our pockets—just one more,

and more, and more.
I stir this feeling into a pot of soup;
living simply is a comfort food.

Economic growth

I thought that I needed
larger pockets
so I could take home
more chestnuts
from my walks
in the woods

but it turns out
it's much better
to just bring someone with me

later
we cooked them together
and ate them with salt
and honey.

Worthy is the fall

The earth into which
my descendants will place their hands
is descending now
from the trees.

Hallelujah—
cling not to your branches;
hallelujah—
worthy is the fall;
hallelujah, hallelujah—
make good the soil.

Harvest Moon

I hold out my cup
before the Harvest Moon,
longing to put my lips
to its silver fruit;

music silks over me
from the clear of the night,
and drinking I am filled
with its sweet, cold light.

Leaf song

You live to drink the sunlight. We all do.
You are hungry for the food
being drawn up by the roots. We all are.
There is life here; you are one;
leaf, branch, bark, trunk.
Who wouldn't
cling on?

Everyone falls; storm-ripped or simply
let go of.
The ground is cold;
you are un-sunned; un-rooted.

It is all decay
for all you know.
It can take years
before you realise
you are soil;
years before you realise
that within you
there is growth.

Glory to the winter's morning

Glory to the winter's morning,
darkling yet nonetheless
eloquent of possibility.

Glory to the fading year, the falling light,
heavy with ending yet nonetheless
dropping hints of beginning.

Glory to slowness, quietude, rest,
so far from what we are taught but nonetheless
so necessary.

Invocation for Advent

Welcome, stranger. Come in. Lay down.
Let us remove this burden of light
that you have carried around for too long.

It is not the darkness that has blinded you.

But now, free from the glare,
you can let your eyes adjust.
Now, sheltered from al that knowing,
you can sit within the shadows' strange conferring.

Together we will light a candle—
not to vanquish the dark, but to further articulate it.

Here may you find the wisdom of winter.
Here may you unlearn the folly of a life
that always climbs the mountain,
that believes in accumulation,
that does not join God
as she too lies fallow—
as she too opens herself to absence.

Advent carol

1
Music saves me.

To the longing, winter's verses resonate best.
In the frost I am discovered, blood-cheeked and awake.

Crisp mornings; misted breath, choral echoes
feel closer to the truth
than glaring summer days.

Long nights; the door shut; candles burning—
the comfort of slowly, quietly; fuel for reflection,
eased of light.

2
Music saves me. Beauty that releases weeping smiles;
lips on the skin of the real of myself;
soft steps into the heart of God.

When I stop; when I free this breath
and listen; when I calm into the now;

I notice the silvered dance of stars—
I feel the movement within me, bittersweet.

3
Music, like poetry, like the trees
and the Christ and the rising cold moon, brings me
home.

I belong here; here, now. In this moment I am warmly
welcomed. In Then and If and When and even Why
we are invasive.

If only we would see that waiting
is simply learning
to be where we are.

4
I long to be this caring more often,
to make a love of the coming away
from the flare of belief and screen
and endless calls to resent.
I do not know a song thrush with an opinion.

Music saves me.

. . .

What gift, this shivered, tenacious air;
what treasure, this blood that still so adores
my continuation; what miracle, this life.

Hope, despite the world and its distractions,
its attempts to tear us from harmony.

5
What stories, what songs did the Magi
slip into their campfires
as brimful of wonder they crossed the desert?
The night sky they would have seen!
Herod, in his palace, was looking only
at his own works.

Have you noticed, longing ones, the beauty
that releases weeping smiles;
slow steps calming into now?
We belong; hope is in the harmonics;
the sky-Christ, your blood! Your blood.

Music saves me.

In the dark

Light is far more eloquent
in the dark,
when we sit beneath the lessons
of the stars,
when we listen to the story
of a lone candle,
and by not seeing everything
we discover
something new.

Winter now your soul

Winter now your soul. Make good of the cold.
Do not carry on as normal—
as though the long nights were not telling you
to fold into your roots, to quit your reaching,
to clear your schedule and curl
into a ritual of hushening ease.

Winter now your soul. Make good of the cold.
There is no use in clinging on—
let yourself let go; settle into deep sighs
under thick blankets, the candles summoning
dulcet shadows on the wall. Empty is not devoid;
it is the space to breathe, the hollow for the seed,
the sanctuary in which you can slowly
regather yourself.

Spell for the winter solstice

Spirit of the long night, solstice angels
so lovingly far from dawn—
hear us now in the nether-light,
dwell us fulsomely in this dark of patience;

here let there be a home for the rest-longing—
for the ones who are tired
of the endless undertow of sun,
done with the striving to make a mark on our days.

Christmas carol

Awake now my love—
the bells of life
are sounding through the frost.
Awake now my love—
the lowly are telling stories
of bright strangers in the hills.
Awake now my love—
the divine is singing longingly
of what it means to be you.

Make now your humble door—
the star-drunk pilgrims
are not looking for a palace.
Gather now the crowns
of bloodberry and green—
the Christ smells of sap
and wet bonfire smoke.
Ready now your journey
from the desolate before—
the mother of the new is in labour;
awake now, and be born.

Epiphany

If tonight, among all the questions,
all the yearnings of your life, there was a star—
strange, haunting, calling
some ancient name—would you know it?

God, oftentimes, is blissfully idle
(and who could blame her,
when there are woods and fields
to stroll in, when the earth is clearly
such an invitation?)
but she is never asleep.
See her now at her leisure, casting impish spells,
laughing shimmers into the high night.

Stir your heart, dearest one.
Give time for your achings
to take in the view.
Something strange, something haunting
is calling out to you.

The cold fields

There is rumour of blackbird song
swimming through the winter-staunch trees.
Night-frosted still, the morning
slowly pulls itself together, horizon aglow.

Paying attention to it, you see
that the world is ever more lovely
than we would ever dare hope.

They tell us not to believe in January;
but here I am, ambling across
the cold fields, smiling.

Coda

RETURN

How to write your name in the Book of Life

Remember that you are nothing,
but that reality is aware of you nonetheless.
Remember that it responds to your heartache.

Return to the truth. Remember
that everyone else
is just as beautifully clueless as you.

Wake up to the facts of yourself;
reach into the corners; peer beneath
the tattered rags.
The real you—all those trenches of longing
dug out by loss—no one is pretending
that it is easy.

Returning to the soul hurts,
so of course we would hide from it;
but to spend our days shuffling
through a fog of distraction
would be to never heal.

. . .

Being alive is difficult. Remember
that you are worth the effort.

Return to what makes you fall in love
with the world. Remember
that part of you that makes time leave you
to get on with things, smiling.

You are new;
you are bringing something here;
be audacious with it.

Wake up to the lovely slowness of the earth.
God is a dawdler—always stopping
to gaze at one thing or another.
Return to rest. Return to rhythm.
If you are too busy, rest even more. Remember
how to do it properly.

Remember the impotence of self-sufficiency.
You cannot live without everything else that is living;
without everything else that has lived.

To be alive is to be interdependent,
to be together
with all the other glimmerings of this place.
Remember this entanglement; it is a holy thing;
it should make you wake up to justice.

The repair of the world is personal.

Remember that you are responsible,
that you can always choose
to make amends.

Wake up to the death and resurrection
that is happening each day.

If you really want to know what's going on,
practice radical kindness. Generosity
will lift your head above the confusion;
an open heart
will fill it all with heaven.
Return to love; remember
that it never fails.

Acknowledgements

It takes a village to make a book. So thank you to my village: to all the people who have inspired, guided, pushed, provoked, encouraged and humoured me. Thank you to my friends and family for the love you always show me despite my many quirks, and my tendency to fall into myself when I am working on a project like this. And a special thank you to you (yes, you!) for buying this book. Being an independent artist can be a lonely place; but the support I've received from this little village of poetry lovers has meant that that feeling has never lasted long. Love and peace to you all.

A b o u t t h e a u t h o r

Gideon is a poet, liturgist and environmentalist who lives by a little patch of woodland in Berkshire, England. You will often find him ambling through the countryside, making up imaginary worlds with his daughter, and sipping coffee while scribbling something in one of his too-many notebooks. He has an MA in Creative Writing, and works in the humanitarian sector.